To all the Curly & Confident Girls
that are going to change the world.

ISBN: 978-1-7345572-1-3

Text copyright 2019 by Ona Zoe Oli & Evana Oli
Illustrations copyright included
First Edition

Curly & Confident Publishing
860 Johnson Ferry Road Ste 140-370
Atlanta GA 30342

A division of Beautiful Curly Me LLC.
http://www.beautifulcurlyme.com

BEAUTIFUL *Curly* ME

By Ona Zoe Oli

Illustrated by Giedre Sen

Stay beautiful! ♡ zoe

CURLY + CONFIDENT
publishing

beautiful

I am beautiful.

Beautiful means I am unique
Created special, to do mighty things.

I may not look like you or I may
We are all beautiful in our own way.

Like the vibrant colors of the rainbow
or ice cream flavors

My peanut butter cocoa skin glows.

I'm *beautiful*.

Beautiful means I am kind
I help those around me every day.

I do nice things to make others smile
I always bring sunshine after the rain.

I'm *beautiful.*

Beautiful means I am strong and fearless
I can do anything I put my mind to, o yes.

I can be anything I want to be
Yes I can, Yes I will.

Yes, I'm *beautiful.*

Beautiful means I am confident
I believe in myself, without a doubt.

I love and accept every part of me
My hair, nose and even the gaps in my teeth.

My mind's so sharp, I love to learn
It's filled with dreams and plans to share.

I always do the best I can
To be a light and show I care.

I'm *beautiful*.

curly

My hair is a basket-full of itty bitty dancing curls

Sometimes big,
Sometimes small,
Never ever dull.

When they are wet, they mosey up
When they are dry, they shimmy out.

Sometimes they wiggle, Sometimes they don't
Sometimes I think my comb makes them giggle.

My curls are magical, oh would you know
One day a fro, the next day cornrows.

Braids, twists, beads, bows
My curls are always the star of the show.

Some friends have hair that's wavy or straight
Others have curls, way different from mine.

Plaits, Hijabs, Buns, Braids
It would be so boring if our hair looked the same.

My curls are big, bold and full of joy
And I am so happy they're mine.

God made my curls pretty, so perfect and free
Unique and truly divine.

me

Me the Strong, Me the Smart, Super Duper Me

I am in the world to do bold amazing things.

I can be
A farmer, A teacher, A chef, A preacher
A mayor, A governor, A lawyer, A doctor.

An engineer, An astronaut, An athlete, An entrepreneur
A firefighter, A writer, A singer or all three.

I can be anything that I want to be
You just wait and see!

Yes, O yes I'm Beautiful
Inside and out, it's true.

Curly, confident
Smart, kind
With a smile that lights up the sky.

I love me. Yes me. Every single part of

beautiful curly me.

Ona Zoe Oli

is the 8 year old CEO of Beautiful Curly Me - an Atlanta-based lifestyle brand that inspires self love & confidence in girls through beautiful black dolls, accessories and hair care products. She is the author of *"Say it, Show it: A Guided Gratitude & Kindness Journal for Kids."*

Zoe is an active 3rd grader who loves reading, art, music and all things STEM. She also enjoys traveling with her family and giving back to the community.

In line with her mission, 10% of all proceeds from this book will go to Girl literacy & empowerment organizations.

Learn more at **BEAUTIFULCURLYME.COM**